26 —

J 598.33

Arctic Tern Migration

by Kari Schuetz

BLASTOFF!
3
READERS

BELLWETHER MEDIA • MINNEAPOLIS, MN

Note to Librarians, Teachers, and Parents:

Blastoff! Readers are carefully developed by literacy experts and combine standards-based content with developmentally appropriate text.

Level 1 provides the most support through repetition of high-frequency words, light text, predictable sentence patterns, and strong visual support.

Level 2 offers early readers a bit more challenge through varied simple sentences, increased text load, and less repetition of high-frequency words.

Level 3 advances early-fluent readers toward fluency through increased text and concept load, less reliance on visuals, longer sentences, and more literary language.

Level 4 builds reading stamina by providing more text per page, increased use of punctuation, greater variation in sentence patterns, and increasingly challenging vocabulary.

Level 5 encourages children to move from "learning to read" to "reading to learn" by providing even more text, varied writing styles, and less familiar topics.

Whichever book is right for your reader, Blastoff! Readers are the perfect books to build confidence and encourage a love of reading that will last a lifetime!

This edition first published in 2019 by Bellwether Media, Inc.

No part of this publication may be reproduced in whole or in part without written permission of the publisher. For information regarding permission, write to Bellwether Media, Inc., Attention: Permissions Department, 6012 Blue Circle Drive, Minnetonka, MN 55343.

Library of Congress Cataloging-in-Publication Data

Names: Schuetz, Kari, author.
Title: Arctic Tern Migration / by Kari Schuetz.
Description: Minneapolis, MN : Bellwether Media, Inc., 2019. | Series:
   Blastoff! Readers. Animals on the Move | Audience: Age 5-8. | Audience:
   Grade K to 3. | Includes bibliographical references and index.
Identifiers: LCCN 2017061811 (print) | LCCN 2018005321 (ebook) | ISBN
   9781626178137 (hardcover : alk. paper) | ISBN 9781681035543 (ebook)
Subjects: LCSH: Arctic tern--Migration--Juvenile literature.
Classification: LCC QL696.C46 (ebook) | LCC QL696.C46 S37 2019 (print) | DDC 598.3/381568--dc23
LC record available at https://lccn.loc.gov/2017061811

Editor: Paige V. Polinsky   Designer: Jeffrey Kollock

Printed in the United States of America, North Mankato, MN

Table of Contents

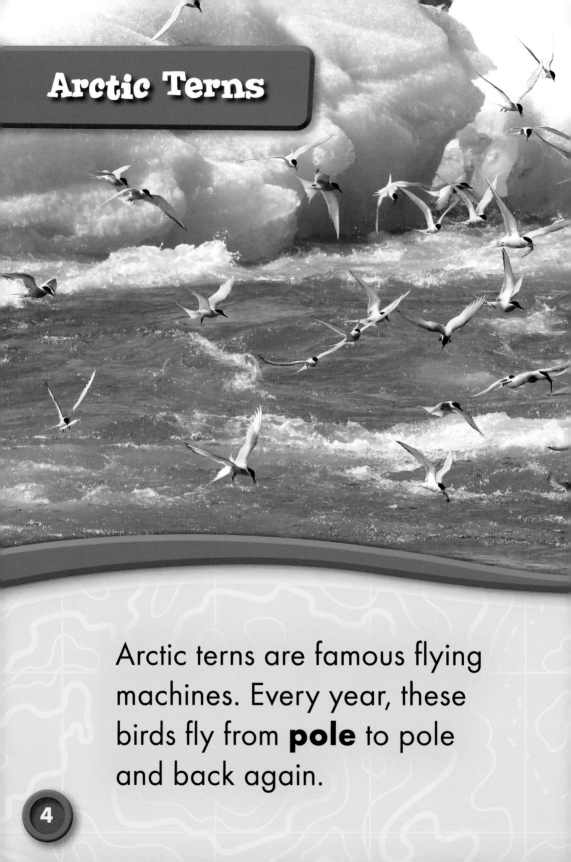

Arctic Terns

Arctic terns are famous flying machines. Every year, these birds fly from **pole** to pole and back again.

Arctic Tern Profile

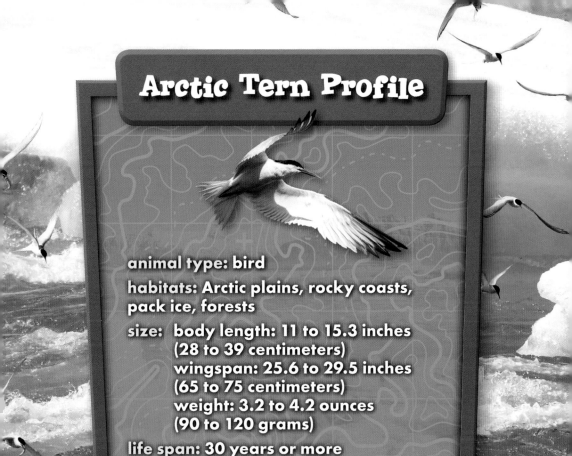

animal type: bird

habitats: Arctic plains, rocky coasts, pack ice, forests

size: body length: 11 to 15.3 inches (28 to 39 centimeters)
wingspan: 25.6 to 29.5 inches (65 to 75 centimeters)
weight: 3.2 to 4.2 ounces (90 to 120 grams)

life span: 30 years or more

This trip is the longest of all animal **migrations**!

Arctic terns are built for life in the air. Their **hollow** bones make them lightweight.

Long, narrow wings allow them to **glide** and **hover**. These special flying skills make long journeys possible.

Arctic winters bring cold, dark days. It becomes harder to fly and fish.

By August or September, the birds are ready to fly south. Summer is just beginning down in the **Antarctic**!

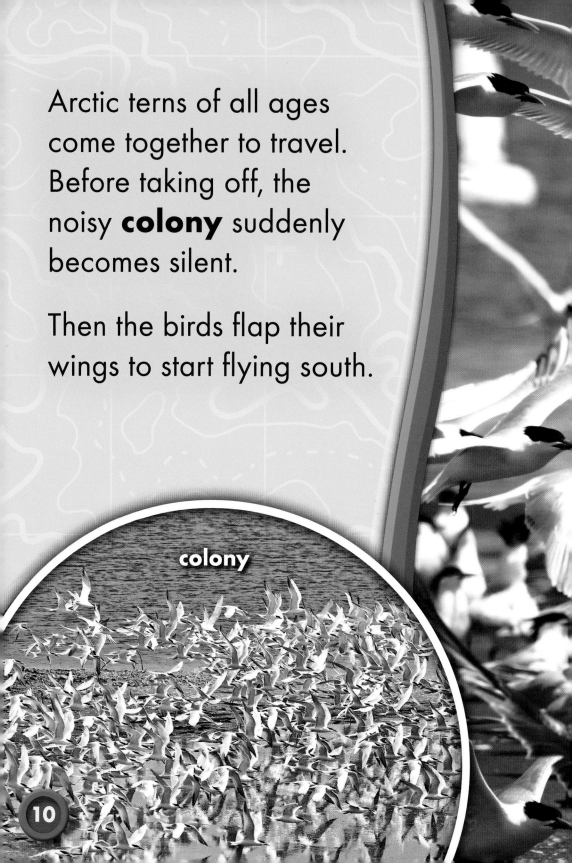

Arctic terns of all ages come together to travel. Before taking off, the noisy **colony** suddenly becomes silent.

Then the birds flap their wings to start flying south.

colony

Arctic Tern Departure

mode of travel: flying

leaving
August/September:
Arctic coast and plains

arriving
November:
Antarctic pack ice

11

Flying South

Arctic terns do not follow a straight path. They **zigzag** between **continents** to fly with the wind.

This requires less effort than flying into the wind. But big storms can throw the birds off course.

On the way south, Arctic terns stop over the North Atlantic Ocean. The birds fish there for almost a month.

Arctic Tern Dashboard

speed: about 25 mph (40 km/h)

mph = miles per hour km/h = kilometers per hour

miles traveled per year:

| 4 | 4 | 0 | 0 | 0 |

(70,811 kilometers)

miles traveled per day:

| - | - | 3 | 2 | 3 |

(520 kilometers)

Then they continue on their trip.
They are able to sleep during flight.

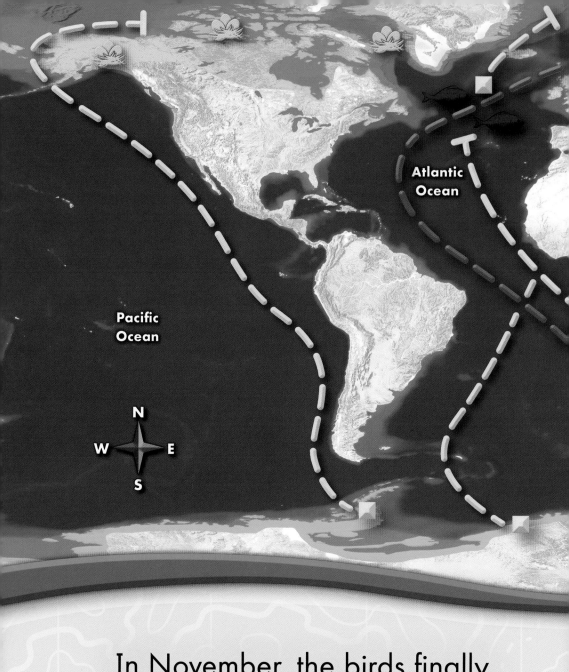

Atlantic
Ocean

Pacific
Ocean

N
W   E
S

In November, the birds finally
reach the Antarctic. This is
where they take a long break
from flying.

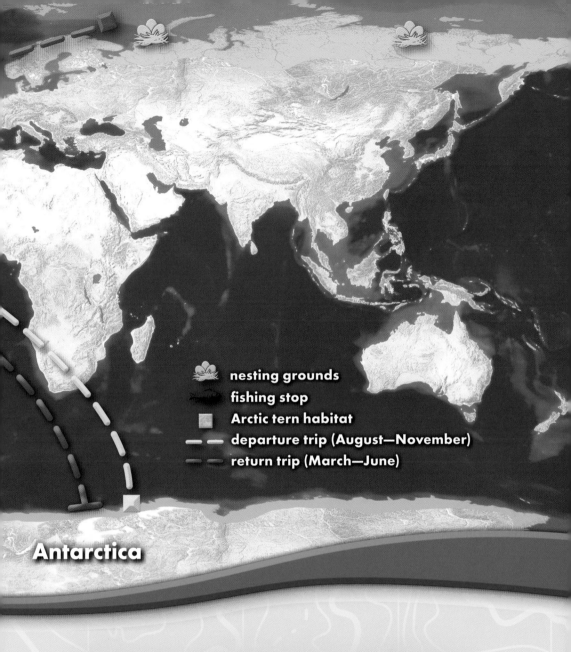

nesting grounds
fishing stop
Arctic tern habitat
departure trip (August—November)
return trip (March—June)

Antarctica

They spend their time fishing and resting on **pack ice**. They also **molt** their feathers.

Back to the Arctic

Young Arctic terns stay in the
Antarctic for two more years.
Adults leave in March or April.

They fly back north to pair up and nest for the summer. The north makes a safe **nursery**.

chick

Back in the Arctic, males charm females with gifts of fish. Each pair makes a ground nest where the female lays eggs.

They wait almost a month for **chicks** to **hatch**. Soon these babies will fly across the world!

eggs

Arctic Tern Return

mode of travel: **flying**

arriving
May/June:
Arctic coast and plains

leaving
March/April:
Antarctic pack ice

Glossary

Antarctic—the area around the South Pole

Arctic—related to the area around the North Pole

chicks—baby Arctic terns

colony—a group of Arctic terns

continents—the seven main areas of land on Earth

glide—to fly through the air smoothly without flapping wings

hatch—to break out of an egg

hollow—empty on the inside

hover—to stay in one spot in midair

migrations—acts of traveling from one place to another, often with the seasons

molt—to lose feathers in order to make room for new ones

nursery—a place where young animals are raised

pack ice—pieces of ice that float together in a cold ocean

pole—either the northernmost or southernmost point of Earth

zigzag—to move in a path with a series of sharp turns

To Learn More

AT THE LIBRARY

Davies, Monika. *How Far Home?: Animal Migrations.*
Mankato, Minn.: Amicus Illustrated, 2019.

Markle, Sandra. *The Long, Long Journey:
The Godwit's Amazing Migration.* Minneapolis, Minn.:
Millbrook Press, 2013.

Tunby, Benjamin. *The Arctic Tern's Journey.* Minneapolis,
Minn.: Lerner Publications, 2018.

ON THE WEB

Learning more about
Arctic tern migration
is as easy as 1, 2, 3.

1. Go to www.factsurfer.com.

2. Enter "Arctic tern migration" into the search box.

3. Click the "Surf" button and you will see a
   list of related web sites.

With factsurfer.com, finding more information
is just a click away.

Index

The images in this book are reproduced through the courtesy of: Dave Head, front cover (bird); Maridav, front cover (background); Frank Fichtmueller, pp. 4-5; aarondfrench, p. 5; Alexandra Giese, p. 6; Mark Medcalf, p. 7; Jakub Mrocek, p. 8; Ondrej Prosicky, p. 9; Philip Pilosian, p. 10; BrooksElliott, pp. 10-11; tahir abbas, p. 12; Oskari Porkka, p. 13; Arto Hakola, p. 14, MyImages_Micha, p. 18; francesco de marco, p. 19; Curioso, p. 20; Joop Zandbergen, pp. 20-21.